Black vultures (Coragyps atratus) *feed on the carcass of an opossum.*

If someone had told that woman that her "eagle" was a vulture, she would have been very disappointed. Vultures just aren't loved and admired the way eagles are. Yet vultures are fascinating birds, and they are among the most im-portant **scavengers**, animals that feed upon the dead bodies of other animals. Vultures help prevent the spread of some diseases by eating up **carcasses,** the bod-ies of dead animals, and in some places, even garbage.

VULTURES

VULTURES

by Lynn M. Stone

A Carolrhoda Nature Watch Book

Carolrhoda Books, Inc./Minneapolis

Photo credits

All photographs © Lynn M. Stone except: pp. 21, 31 (both) © Joe McDonald; p. 26, © Andrea Gaski/Ron Tilson;
p. 32, Walt Anderson; p. 33, © John Flower; pp. 36, 37, 38, Ron Garrison/© Zoological Society of San Diego;
p. 40, P. J. Mundy.

To learn more about vultures and their conservation, contact:

Vulture Study Group
c/o The Center for the Study of Tropical Birds
218 Conway Drive
San Antonio, TX 78209-1716.

LIBRARY OF CONGRESS CATALOGING-IN-PUBLICATION DATA

Stone, Lynn M.
    Vultures / by Lynn M. Stone.
        p.   cm.
    "A Carolrhoda nature watch book."
    Includes index.
    Summary: Describes the life cycle, habitats, and reputation of
both Old and New World vultures.
    ISBN 0-87614-768-6
    1. Vultures—Juvenile literature. [1. Vultures.] I. Title.
QL696.F3S77   1993
598'.912—dc20   92-26721
                                                   CIP
                                                    AC

Manufactured in the United States of America

1 2 3 4 5 6 98 97 96 95 94 93

For Kathryn, whose dad is raising vultures as well as a daughter

Thanks to Dr. Jack C. Eitniear for his assistance with this book. Thanks to the following for their photographic assistance: The Alpenzoo, Innsbruck, Austria; The Center for the Study of Tropical Birds, San Antonio, Texas; The Chicago Zoological Park (Brookfield Zoo), Brookfield, Illinois; The San Diego Wild Animal Park, San Diego, California; and Weeki Wachee Spring, Weeki Wachee, Florida.

A turkey vulture (Cathartes aura)

The woman standing by the shore of the Florida lake studied the big, brownish black bird perched nearby on a dead tree limb. The bird had a bald red head and a hooked beak. With the voice of someone who knew what she was talking about, she said to her companion, "There's a bald eagle!"

The bird was bald all right, but it wasn't an eagle. It was a turkey vulture. The turkey vulture's head is without feathers. An adult bald eagle's head is covered with white feathers. Like a bald eagle, however, a turkey vulture is a large, dark-bodied bird with long, broad wings for soaring and a sharp, hooked beak for tearing flesh. Like other kinds of vultures, it shares the eagle's taste for meat, and the eagle's great eyesight. As you might suspect, the eagle and vulture are related. And sometimes, as happened along that lakeshore, vultures are mistaken for eagles.

Because vultures feed on dead things, or **carrion,** people connect vultures with death. Actually, vultures rarely cause an animal's death. They just feed upon animals that have been killed by people, automobiles, disease, disasters, or **predators,** the hunting animals.

However, animals that kill for themselves seem to command greater respect than scavengers. People often forget—or don't know—that many predators eat carrion, too. Eagles, for instance, are skillful hunters, but they often dine on animals that they did not kill.

Although known as excellent hunters, bald eagles will also feed on carrion if it's available.

The bald eagle (top) *and the peregrine falcon* (bottom) *are both raptors, as are vultures.*

The vultures of the world do not have the regal looks of eagles. Unless they're being served for dinner, birds are supposed to be covered with feathers. But most vultures have heads nearly as bare as pickles. Some kinds of vultures have bare necks to match. The vulture's naked head and the hunched way it perches are largely responsible for the "vulture look." If an eagle looks like it was made for a royal throne, a vulture looks like it was made for a Halloween party. Still, vultures share common ground with eagles, as well as hawks, kites, buzzards, falcons, and caracaras, all of which are birds of prey, or **raptors**. Some raptors belong to the scientific **order**, or group, known as Falconiformes.

The word *raptor* comes from a Latin word that means "to take and carry away." The raptors include **diurnal** birds of prey—those that are active during the day—and owls, most of which are **nocturnal**, or active at night.

10

Above: *Vultures' talons are not as strong as those of other raptors.* Below: *A black vulture* (left) *perches alongside a turkey vulture* (right).

Like other raptors, vultures have hooked bills, and feet with **talons**. A talon is a sharp claw that extends from each of four toes. Some raptors have longer, sharper, and stronger talons than others. Talons are used by most raptors to grasp and kill **prey**, the animals they hunt. But vultures' weak feet are more useful for hopping than for killing. In fact, a vulture's foot is often compared to a chicken's foot. So without powerful feet to strike prey, vultures eat leftovers.

Vultures' lack of hunting skill helps separate them from hawks, eagles, and other birds of prey. Another way in which vultures differ from other raptors is in the size of males and females. Among many birds of prey, females are much larger than their mates. Male and female vultures, however, are about the same size. Vultures are more social than other raptors, too. Groups of vultures often feed, fly, and roost together.

Ornithologists, scientists who study birds, place the different types of vultures in two separate groups. Fifteen **species**, or kinds, of vultures live in Africa, Asia, and Europe. Ornithologists call that group the Old World vultures. Old World vultures belong to the family called Accipitridae, within the order Falconiformes. Seven species of so-called New World vultures live in North and South America. These vultures of the Americas include two supersized models known as condors. New World vultures make up the family Cathartidae in the order Ciconiiformes, which also includes such long-legged birds as herons, egrets, and storks.

Scientists who study the skeletons and habits of birds think that the two modern groups of vultures **evolved**, or developed, from ancestors in two quite different groups of birds. In other words, Old World vultures were once much more like hawks, but during the passage of thousands of years, they slowly became what they are today. But New World vultures have evolved—again, during a period of thousands of years—from the storks, many of which also have bare heads and feed on carrion.

The lappet-faced vulture (above) *is one of the Old World vultures, while the turkey vulture* (opposite page, left) *is an example of a New World vulture. New World vultures are descended from the same ancestors as modern storks, such as the marabou stork* (opposite page, right).

12

Both groups of modern vultures have similar lifestyles—they are scavengers. And although the Old and New World vulture groups were separated by oceans, the birds developed similar special features called **adaptations**. Adaptations enable an animal to do what it must in order to survive in nature. The vultures' best-known adaptation is the bareness or partial bareness of the head and neck. Featherless areas help a vulture to stay reasonably clean and, therefore, healthy. A vulture's head is often soaked in blood and flesh from the carcasses it eats. Instead of having bloody head feathers to clean and dry, a vulture has to deal only with drying its skin. The sun takes care of that. Sunshine not only dries the skin, it kills **bacteria**, microscopic organisms that are among those we commonly call germs. Bacteria feed on dead animals and cause many diseases in both people and animals. Bacteria are more likely to grow in damp feathers than on bare, easily dried skin.

Vultures' long, bare necks help them survive as scavengers.

The vulture's neck itself seems to be another adaptation to a life of scavenging. A vulture's neck is something like a turkey's, long and slender. This allows a vulture to poke its head deeply into a carcass without having to take its entire body along.

Vultures usually locate food by hunting from great heights. They either see the food, using their excellent eyesight, or they see the activity of other animals that signals the presence of food. In either case, vultures need to be able to fly high and sometimes remain in flight for a long time. Vultures' long, wide wings are adapted for the job. Basically vultures are soaring birds. They sail on outstretched wings and seldom flap their wings. They can hold their place in the sky, or rise or fall as they wish, with very little effort. Just as a kite on a string rises easily with wind currents, so too does a vulture.

A Rüppell's griffon vulture (Gyps ruepellii) *in flight*

Vultures and other birds have light, hollow bones as an adaptation for flight. The lighter a bird is, and the bigger its wings in comparison to its body size, the easier it can become airborne. Compared to their body size, vultures have large wings. Those big wings give a vulture tremendous lift, and when air currents are favorable, most vultures take off easily from the ground or a perch. Aloft, the vulture is a magnificent soarer. Unlike handmade kites, vultures have command of their flight.

Even when it is flapping its wings, a large vulture averages only 1 wing beat per second. Small hawks average 2 to 3 wing beats each second. Most small birds average 30 to 80 wing beats per second. Such relaxed flying by vultures doesn't produce great speed, but it doesn't waste energy either. For a bird that may not find food each day, conserving body energy is important. Anyway, a vulture doesn't need exceptional flight speed. Being able to soar and carefully study the land below is more useful for a vulture than being able to rocket downward like a falcon. After all, a vulture's prey is in no position to run away!

If vultures' outsides have adapted to a life of scavenging, so have their insides. Eating garbage and diseased flesh could be dangerous to a bird's health. Vultures' digestive systems—where food is processed and passed—solve the problem. The digestive systems of vultures seem to destroy even the most dangerous forms of bacteria.

The vultures of worlds Old and New have their differences as well as their similarities. Look at their heads, for instance. New World vultures have open, see-through nostrils in their beaks. You won't see a thing through the nostrils of Old World vultures. And look at the eyes. Many of the Old World vultures have an eaglelike ridge over their eyes. They look fierce. New World vultures don't have the ridge, so they appear round-eyed and good-natured. There are differences in nesting habits, too. Beyond that, most of the differences between vultures of the Old World and the New are internal—differences that are within the birds.

New World vultures, such as the king vulture pictured on the opposite page, have see-through nostrils in their beaks. Notice the ridge above the eye of the Old World cinereous vulture at left.

Turkey vultures, unlike most vultures, fly south when the weather turns cool.

Vultures large and small are found in certain parts of the Americas, Asia, Africa, and Europe, usually around open and semi-open countryside. Vultures are found in many kinds of areas, or **habitats**, along sea coasts, over deserts and dry plains, above partly forested lands, and around mountain peaks up to 25,000 feet (7,620 meters) above the sea. Vultures of one kind or another live from the world's warm tropical regions north into southern Canada and southern Russia. Most vultures stay in their favorite area year-round. Several types of birds, such as ducks and geese, **migrate**. They travel each spring from a mild wintering ground to a northern summer home. Each fall, they return southward. But vultures tend to be homebodies. One exception is the turkey vulture. The turkey vultures that spend summers in southern Canada and the northern United States fly into the southern states each fall.

The turkey vultures that fly into Hinckley, Ohio, each March are met with enthusiasm by hundreds of people on Buzzard Day. ("Buzzard" is an inaccurate but nevertheless common term for vultures in North America. True buzzards are a kind of Old World raptor.)

Most people think of vultures as all alike. But there are 22 different kinds of vultures, and they are a mixed lot. Take size, for example. One of the smallest vultures, the common turkey vulture, has a six-foot (1.8 m) **wingspan**, the distance from the tip of one of the bird's outstretched wings to the tip of the other. The great condors have wingspans of about 10 feet (3 m). A condor may weigh 30 pounds (13.5 kg), although 25 (11.25) is more typical. The Himalayan griffon vulture and cinereous vulture are also heavyweights, sometimes weighing nearly 25 pounds (11.25 kg). In comparison, the turkey vulture weighs less than 5 pounds (2.25 kg).

The Andean condor (Vultur gryphus) *has an enormous wingspan.*

Most vultures are rather unusual-looking. The colorful king vulture (above) and the Andean condor *(opposite page)* both have growths called caruncles on their beaks.

Vultures are "supposed" to be brown or black. Many of them are. Yet some vultures, such as the adult Egyptian vulture, are mostly white. Vulture heads and necks are no less surprising. They come in paint store colors: red, yellow, black, orange, white, brown, gray, and combinations. The king vulture of Mexico and South America rivals a circus poster. It has a fleshy red growth, called a wattle or caruncle, above its nostrils, and a red circle around its white eye. Its head and neck are a mix of yellow, orange, purple, and blue. It wears a collar of gray feathers and has a largely white body with black-trimmed white wings.

Another vulture of distinction is the king's larger cousin, the Andean condor. The male Andean condor has a large caruncle on its bill, and black-and-white **plumage** (feathers). The skin along the sides of its head and throat forms long, loose folds known as lappets.

As a group, birds are not blessed with a keen sense of smell. Like other birds, vultures are never going to replace bloodhounds. Curiously, though, the turkey vulture has a "good nose." It seems to be the only vulture capable of finding an animal carcass by smelling it. The turkey vulture's sharp sense of smell may explain why these birds are often seen in low-level flights. A vulture cruising low cannot see as much ground as a high, soaring vulture. But if the vulture can smell a meal hidden on the ground, it doesn't have to see it first.

Rüppell's griffon vultures dining on the body of a wildebeest

Exactly what a vulture eats depends somewhat upon the kind of vulture that is doing the eating, and where it is hunting. On the whole, vultures eat old flesh. Occasionally, vultures spice their diet with fresh meat or plant matter—fruits and vegetables. The American black vulture, for example, will kill baby birds or other small, helpless animals. Some of the larger vultures probably kill helpless young mammals—lambs and calves, for instance—that are sick and unable to run.

Vultures eat human flesh when they have the opportunity. In the mountainous nation of Tibet and in the city of Bombay, India, vultures are encouraged to feed on human corpses. In rocky Tibet, the burial of corpses is difficult. That fact, along with local beliefs, has helped establish the tradition of placing human bodies outdoors to be eaten by vultures. In India, the Zoroastrians, a religious group, believe that vultures were created to consume the dead. In this way, they believe, vultures help keep the earth's pure soil and water free of death's pollution.

This wildebeest carcass has been picked clean by vultures.

This Egyptian vulture (Neophron percnopterus) *holds a stone, which it is about to drop on the egg.*

A vulture with most curious tastes is the bearded vulture, found in parts of Europe, Africa, and Asia, and known in Europe as the lammergeier. This bird eats bones! It will swallow whole bones if they're small enough. But the bearded vulture also likes bone marrow, the soft substance inside bones. The trick is being able to reach the marrow inside bones that are too large to swallow. Since the vulture's beak and feet are not strong enough to smash bones, the bearded vulture will carry a bone into the air and drop it onto rocks until the bone splits open. Once the marrow has been exposed, the bearded vulture removes it with its rough tongue.

The Egyptian vulture of Africa also has a unique feeding habit. Fond of ostrich eggs, the Egyptian vulture has become a "pitcher." The shell of an ostrich egg is too strong for an Egyptian vulture to crack. But a tough eggshell does not keep this remarkable bird from a meal. The bird picks up a stone in its bill and hurls it toward the egg. Eventually a stone finds the target and cracks the eggshell.

Different vulture species often feed together. Here, Rüppell's griffon vultures share a wildebeest carcass with African white-backed vultures.

The palm nut vulture of Africa is something of an outcast in the society of vultures. First, it looks amazingly like an eagle, enough so that is sometimes called the vulturine fish eagle. Second, it has a very unvulturelike diet. Its preferred food is the husk that covers the fruits of oil palms and raffia palms.

Vultures often feed together in large numbers. Other birds of prey generally kill for themselves or their chicks. But because a large animal—a zebra or a cow, perhaps—will feed many vultures, it is first come, first served in the vulture world.

Competition among vultures at a carcass can be fierce. A carcass may disappear under a blanket of hungry vultures. Wings flap, bills jab, and the birds squabble in a chorus of grunts, croaks, and hisses. A large vulture can eat over two pounds of meat in two minutes. Birds don't chew; they swallow chunks of meat whole. Vultures can clean the meet off a young African antelope in half an hour. After the biggest vultures eat their fill, smaller vultures pick scraps and nip the last traces of flesh from the skeleton. The hooded vulture, for example, has a long, slender bill perfectly adapted for snipping the last tiny scraps of meat from bones.

Settling onto a carcass, vultures are an unruly lot. The only rule at the "table" seems to be that the biggest, oldest, and hungriest vultures eat first, wherever they can find a place to grab a bite. Usually, the larger species of vultures at a carcass chase smaller vultures away by lunging toward them with open wings and jabbing bills. Newcomers to the feast use the same threatening gestures to drive away vultures that have already begun to fill up. Scientists call this bullying behavior a threat display.

Vultures must compete for food not only with other vultures, but also with larger predators. Here, a spotted hyena chases white-backed vultures from a carcass.

Vultures wouldn't survive, of course, without food. Neither would they survive without creating more vultures. The most important time in the vulture's year is the nesting season. After all, the future of the vulture depends upon the successful hatching of eggs and the raising of young.

The timing of the nesting season depends upon the species of vulture and where it lives. The American black vultures that live in the southeastern United States may begin nesting as early as January or as late as April. In Argentina, the same species may begin nesting in November.

Before nesting actually begins, many vultures engage in various kinds of courtship behavior. That may involve some strutting, bowing, and even hopping about—vulture "dancing." In some species, courtship involves spectacular flights. Pairs of bearded vultures and Indian black vultures, for instance, participate in breathtaking dives and rolls, like matched pairs of combat aircraft.

Although social birds, most pairs of vultures nest apart from other vultures. Old World vultures usually build nests of sticks. The nest may be on the ground, or well aboveground in a tree or on a ledge. New World vultures have a completely different idea of nest building—they don't do it. Like various seabirds—puffins, penguins, gannets, and murres among them—New World vultures don't build nests. Instead, they find flat spots on the ground, usually well hidden, or hollows in trees, and lay their eggs there.

In most cases, vultures lay two eggs, though condors and king vultures lay only one. Vulture parents, male and female alike, share the task of **incubating**, keeping the eggs warm and the tiny chick inside alive. Incubation generally takes five to seven weeks, larger species taking longer than smaller species.

An Andean condor at a nest site.

A lappet-faced vulture chick (left) *and parent at their nest.*

A newborn turkey vulture alongside one in the process of hatching. Notice the egg tooth breaking through the shell.

A baby vulture begins to chip its way out of the egg with the help of a horn-like growth on its upper beak. Called an egg tooth, the growth falls off soon after the chick hatches. The hatching process usually takes more than a full day.

Baby vultures are helpless at birth. Covered only by a thin down, they rely on their parents for warmth and food. The parents take turns with feeding and **brooding**, or using their bodies to keep the chicks warm until they can control their own body temperatures.

Vultures are not well equipped to transport food, except in their bellies. The weak vulture feet cannot grasp and carry meat to a nest. Young eagles and hawks grow up on pieces of flesh that their parents tear from prey carried to the nest. Vulture chicks, in contrast, grow up on partially digested food that their parents **regurgitate**, or throw up, into the nest. Vultures, it appears, develop a taste for "secondhand" food early in life.

A black vulture chick

A young Andean condor

Vulture chicks stay in or near the nest site until they learn to fly, or **fledge**. Larger vulture species take longer to grow up than smaller species. The American black vulture and turkey vulture, both of which are fairly small, are nest-bound for about 2½ months before they have flight feathers. Young Andean and California condors have an exceptionally long "childhood" for birds. Many large birds, such as geese and swans, fly within a few weeks after hatching. Born in late June, Arctic geese and swans fly south on long journeys in September. Condors, on the other hand, begin flying at seven months of age. Even then, they are not ready for life alone. They return to the nest site and are sometimes fed by the adults until they are more than a year old! Because of this long "childhood," adult condors nest only every other year.

Old condors certainly do not make new condors quickly. Still, condors were able to keep their populations steady for many thousands of years. The birds lived to an old age, perhaps 25 or 30 years. They had few natural enemies, and they lived in rugged country, where people rarely ventured. The condors were fairly safe. Some condors were killed by native North and South American peoples, but condor populations as a whole suffered little from this hunting. When native people did capture and kill condors, it was mostly because they believed that condors' feathers and body parts had supernatural powers. In one California tribe, condor feathers were sometimes pushed into the throats of sick people. The feathers were supposed to help cure disease.

In recent generations, the world's human population has grown tremendously. Villages, cities, and farms exist where there were unsettled, wild lands before. With more people come changes in the environment, and most of the changes do not help wildlife.

There are few condors left in the wild. Many, including this Andean condor, live in zoos.

The condors of North and South America have fared poorly. Both are recognized as endangered species along with two other vulture species, the cinereous vulture of Eurasia and the cape griffon vulture of South Africa. Endangered animals are threatened with the possibility of disappearing forever, or becoming **extinct**. The California condor is especially endangered. It is one of the rarest birds in the world.

The California condor was never common, but by 1986 its troubles had pushed it nearly to extinction. One cause of the California condors' shrinking population was lead poisoning. The condors sometimes fed upon the remains of game animals killed by lead bullets. When the condors fed upon dead farm animals, some of them died from poisons that ranchers and government agents had put in the carcasses to kill another scavenger, the coyote. And although it was against the law, hunters shot some California condors.

A California condor chick (Gymnogyps californianus), *born in the special captive breeding program at the San Diego Wild Animal Park.*

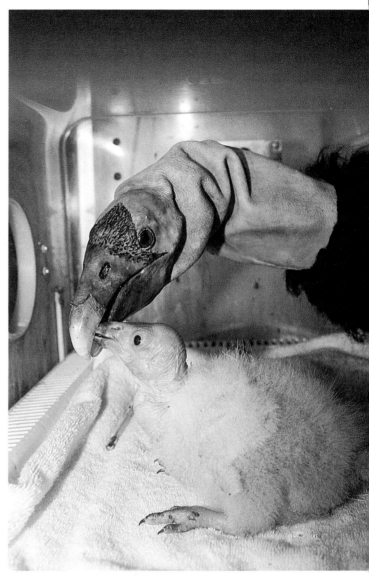

In a captive breeding program, puppets that look like California condor parents are used to feed the chicks.

Faced with the knowledge that California condors were dying faster than they could ever reproduce, the United States Fish and Wildlife Service in 1986 ordered that the last few wild condors be captured. The last wild California condor was trapped in April of 1987. Like others that had already been taken from the wild, this bird was placed in a captive breeding program. In a captive breeding program, wild animal species are bred in a zoo or some other controlled setting to build up their populations. California condors are now being bred at both the Los Angeles Zoo and the San Diego Wild Animal Park, both in Southern California.

The success of captive breeding means that California condors such as this one may be able to survive in the wild.

The Fish and Wildlife Service's California Condor Recovery Plan had hoped to begin releasing condors back into the wild by 1993. The unexpected success in breeding captive condors, however, led to the release of a pair of condors in the fall of 1991. Another 50 California condors, all that is left of this entire species, remained in captivity. The recovery program hopes to eventually establish two groups of wild condors, each numbering about 100 birds.

The cinereous vulture, found in parts of Europe and Asia, is in danger of becoming extinct.

In addition to the California condor, other species of vultures have been reduced by changes in the way land is used, changing populations of wild animals, and shooting by hunters. Like all birds of prey, vultures are protected by law in Mexico, Canada, and the United States. North American countries view raptors as valuable pieces of the whole puzzle of plants and animals that makes up the natural system. Hawks, eagles, and owls kill huge numbers of rodents, and vultures clean up dead animals. All play an important part in keeping nature in balance. Protection by law doesn't prevent all killing of raptors by gunfire, however. In some countries outside of North America, hunting is a major problem.

For many species of vultures, the change of wild lands to town and farm has destroyed some nesting, feeding, and roosting areas. Human use of the land has also had an impact on the ability of some vultures to find food. When farm animals die in fields, they are often removed by people before scavengers can feed upon them. Even when carcasses are left, they may be harmful to the raptors that eat them. Golden eagles, as well as California condors, have died from consuming poisoned carcasses. In South Africa, the cape griffon once lived on the bodies of wild animals that had been torn and ripped by predators. The bone fragments of these carcasses provided calcium for the birds. Calcium is a natural substance that helps build strong bones. When farmers killed off the predators, there were no more torn, broken carcasses. The griffons settled for the whole carcasses of sheep and cattle that had died of natural causes. But apparently the griffons could not obtain bone fragments small enough to eat. Without bones in their diets, baby griffons began to develop problems with the formation of their own bones.

Cape griffon vultures (above and opposite page) *have been affected by human use of their habitats.*

A bearded vulture (Gypaetus barbatus)

Scientists suspected the cause of the problem and did something about it. Feeding stations were created for griffons. Now cape griffons can scavenge on carcasses with broken bones, placed there by scientists who want to help the birds recover and survive. Vulture restaurants like the ones in South Africa have also been used to assist bearded vultures in Europe and condors in California.

Being a vulture means being able to eat just about anything that once crawled, swam, ran, or—yes—drove a car. That kind of flexibility toward food has its advantages. But being a vulture is not especially easy. A vulture's life is filled with danger. People with rifles sometimes make these wide-winged birds their targets. Autos speeding past vultures feeding at road kills strike the vultures that fail to hop or fly quickly away, and the carrion eater becomes carrion itself.

There are other dangers: unseen utility wires that bring soaring vultures twisting and crashing down, and the poisoned carcasses used to bait coyotes, so tempting to a vulture but so deadly. The vulture's stomach of steel can whip germs, but it doesn't stand a chance against chemical potions brewed up in a laboratory.

For some people, a vulture will always be a creature of evil eyes, Death on wings, a hunched bird with a hooked beak waiting for a weary traveler to lie down in the dust and die. More enlightened people have increasingly begun to see vultures as helpful scavengers and a fascinating part of our planet's bird life.

Vultures are tough, like the bones they crack and the leathery old hides they tear. And they are wonderfully adapted for searching and finding a morsel here and there to tide them over until the next morsel. But in a world that we are rapidly changing in ways that rarely benefit wildlife, vultures need a bit of help and understanding. Then, we can be sure they will continue to dazzle us with their mastery of flight—and continue to shock us with their choice of desserts.

Vultures have cleaned the rotting flesh from this wildebeest's skull, keeping disease-causing bacteria from growing.

GLOSSARY

adaptations: a special feature or characteristic, such as a vulture's bare head, that enables an organism to better survive in its habitat

bacteria: a group of microscopic organisms, some of which cause certain diseases

brooding: warming eggs or young birds in a nest

carcasses: the dead bodies of animals

carrion: dead, rotting flesh

diurnal: active in the daytime

evolved: developed over a long period of time

extinct: no longer in existence

fledge: to develop the right feathers for flight

habitats: the specific areas where animals live

incubating: keeping the eggs in a nest warm until they hatch

migrate: to move from one location to another, usually to reach new feeding grounds

nocturnal: active at night

order: a scientific grouping of animals that have some features in common

ornithologists: scientists who study birds

plumage: a bird's covering of feathers

predators: animals that hunt and kill other animals for food

prey: animals that are killed and eaten by other animals

raptors: the birds of prey, including owls, hawks, eagles, and vultures

regurgitate: to throw up partially digested food, often for the purpose of feeding young

scavengers: animals that feed on the dead bodies of other animals

species: a specific kind of animal within a larger scientific grouping of similar animals, for example, a *king* vulture

talons: the sharp claws on the feet of birds of prey

wingspan: the distance across a bird's outstretched wings, from one wing tip to the other

INDEX

ABOUT THE AUTHOR

Lynn M. Stone is an author and photographer who has written more than 120 books for young readers about wildlife and natural history. In addition to photographing wildlife, Mr. Stone enjoys fishing and travel. A former teacher, he lives with his wife and daughter in Batavia, Illinois.